E. D Rand, Association Lisbon Library

Poems and Selections

E. D Rand, Association Lisbon Library

Poems and Selections

ISBN/EAN: 9783744711029

Printed in Europe, USA, Canada, Australia, Japan

Cover: Foto ©Thomas Meinert / pixelio.de

More available books at **www.hansebooks.com**

POEMS

AND

SELECTIONS

BY

E. D. RAND.

PUBLISHED BY "LISBON LIBRARY ASSOCIATION,"
1885.

NOTE.

The following Poems and Selections from the stray literary papers of a busy lawyer, are published as a Memorial of their Author, in obedience to a very general desire of those who knew him most intimately. Some of them are only fragments, without titles even, and without careful and critical revision, the product of a few leisure hours which were snatched from an exacting and laborious profession, and are given as they were left in their incomplete form.

They are published solely in the interest of the "Lisbon Library Association."

CONTENTS.

POEMS.

SELECTIONS.

POEMS.

POEMS.

THE TWO VOICES.

FIRST VOICE.

In all this unresponsive universe,
What canst thou see, O dreamer of fond dreams,
That fills thy heart with hope? Thy little life,
Alas! is but a fiery spark, that drops
Into a shoreless sea — a brief sweet dream,
That fades into a dreamless sleep. The earth
Itself, on which thou standest, vast to thee,
And full of hopeless mystery, the grave
Of unremembered millions of thy race,
Is but a grain of sand,
In yonder starry wilderness of worlds.

And what indeed art thou, that Nature should
Remember aught of thee? Will her rough breast

Grow soft in pity for thy bruised limbs,
Or her great heart beat quick with pain, because
Thine eyes are filled with tears?

On tireless wings
The days and months will pass as swiftly as
A " weaver's shuttle," and the joyless sleep
Which nevermore in all the noiseless years
Can be disturbed, will come, as surely as
Old age must follow youth.   Thy body will
Become a clod, and thy frail spirit but
A wasted breath.

SECOND VOICE.

Lift up thy saddened eyes in hope, thou child
Of God.   Can thought be born of that, which hath
No power of thought?   Whence comes thy won-
        drous soul,
Unless there somewhere be a grander Soul
That touches thine through laws that never change?
The universe is vast indeed; but He

Who planned and made it, fills it through and
    through —
The smallest atom and the largest star,
There is no point in space where Chaos reigns.
Lean then securely on the Eternal Law,
That rests upon the Everlasting Thought,
And underlies all life and death. Take thou
The " Morning's wings," and upward pass beyond
The Pleiades and this shall follow thee,
And be around thee and within. And down
Beneath the sea, the tiniest things that move
In strange and sunless caves, are fashioned with
Minutest care, and live and die in strict
Obedience to a still resistless Power.
Each hair upon thy head, once broken from
Thy life, shall tenderly be handed back
Into the universal life, without
Haste and without waste. Fearest thou that that
Which is thy very self — thy soul — with its
Prophetic and far-reaching thought, can be
Forgotten? Fear it not, but strong in hope,

Exultant in thy faith, go forth to meet
The certain Life in Death, as if to meet
A steadfast friend, who waits to welcome thee.
For great, benignant Nature, who in her
Appointed way and time remembers all
Things, must remember thee, and all the seed
Her hand hath scattered, and the harvest of
Immortal fruit.

THRENODY.

Through all the lingering years in vain for thy embrace
An aching heart will yearn and wait ! By day or night
I never — nevermore shall look upon thy face,
Or watch thy cheerful coming with a new delight.
A thousand things will say to me — it is the end
Of life, now in the fullness of good deeds complete.
But what hast thou to fear, my restful, vanished friend,
Since sleep, dreamful or dreamless, either way, is
        sweet ?

BEHIND THE VEIL.

Lo ! the marvellous contrast of shadow and light,—
Of shadows that darken and lights that adorn ;
And after the day comes the shadowy night,
And after the night come the splendors of morn.

And raptures and sorrows through all the brief years
Keep crossing, to weave in the web of our life,
Till another, the greatest of shadows appears,
To hush into stillness the tumult and strife.

And thou, Shadow of shadows, the darkest of all,
Concealing what has been and what is to be,
That liest on life and its joys like a pall,
Oh ! what is the splendor that lies behind thee ?

TRUTH.

There is hope in the clash of creeds,
In the war of the old and new,
And in all the valiant deeds
Of soldiers good and true.
But many eyes must weep,
For human faith is weak,
And Truth is buried deep,
And science slow to speak,
And error well inwrought
With all the forms of thought.
But why indeed should those
(Now toiling in repose)
Who worship only Truth,
Be troubled by the throes
Of an angry world, forsooth?
This only they demand :
That human thought be free
To labor at its task,

And wave its sceptre of command
Over continents of land
And islands of the sea ;—
That truth be not concealed,
And falsehood drop her mask.
Then let the lines be drawn,
The banners be unfurled,
The rival trumpets blown,
And let the war rage on
Until God's will be done
Through all the stormy world.
There is glory in the strife,
For truth can never die,
And only a dying life
Be given to a lie.
The little that we know
Can never pass away,
And more may be revealed.
The solid earth will stay,
The eternal rivers flow
To the eternal sea ;

Nor will the Heavens decay;
Venus and fiery Mars,
And Jupiter the grand,
And all the shining band
Of sweet, familiar stars,
Which now our eyes can see,
In their accustomed places,
In the far, aerial spaces,
Will show their smiling faces;
And beyond all these, no less,
In the blue immensity,
Will glow a wilderness
Of stars we cannot see.

SONNET.

Another joy has gone out of a life,
  As though a moon should drop from its path,
Fall away from a cluster
Of stars, bereaving the sky of its lustre,
  The earth of its glory. Who is there who fears
Not a still, ignominious strife,
  The torture of desolate tears,
  The fires of a smouldering wrath,
  That will burn through the lingering years,
And be quenched in the lethe of death?
  A gloom that can never depart,
Since the light of each pitiless morrow
  Must bring to an o'erburdened heart
A voiceless and measureless sorrow.

IN MEMORIAM.

JAMES A. GARFIELD.

The spirit hath taken its flight,
　Where the land and the waters meet,
And never a nobler fight
　Was crowned with immortal defeat.

O! weak as the opening air,
　To the pressure of death-dealing darts,
Is the burden of innermost prayer,
　From millions of agonized hearts.

And vain is the vigilant skill
　That watches mysterious laws,
And vainer the dominant will,
　That clings to a perishing cause.

Dead! by the murmuring shore
　Of the cold and passionless sea;

O ! brave, noble heart, nevermore,
  Can its voices be music to thee.

Released from the wearisome strife,
  The torture of laboring breath,—
Up into the glory of life,
  That gleams through the shadow of death.

AFTER THE BATTLE.

On the horizon's edge reclining
Ghost-like sits the moon in shrouds.
Here and there the stars are shining
Dimly through the scattered clouds.

Cannon's roar and musket's rattle
Rend no more the startled air ;
Hushed are all the sounds of battle.
Beasts of prey are drawing near.

Friends and foes no longer heeding
Hatred in each other's eyes,
Side by side lie torn and bleeding,
Careless of the victor's prize.

Heroes, wounded, worn and wasted,
Sink upon the ground to-night,
Joys they dreamed of all untasted
Swim before their glazing sight.

Friends at home who loved them fondly,—
Proud of all their former scars,
Who shall tell those friends how soundly
Now they sleep beneath the stars?

Lay them in their beds of glory,
Fast by ocean's sounding waves;
None there are to tell their story,
Yet they sleep in holy graves.

Earth, thou fond and gentle mother,
Fold them on thy loving breast;
Guard them safely till another
Morn shall break their solemn rest.

We pray not for ourselves,—the strife
And pain and doubt will come no more
To us,—and Death is but the door
That opens to a larger life.

We pray for all the souls that grope
In darkness — bear the heavy load
Of doubt upon their weary road,
And never feel the joy of hope.

OH! WHY ARE THE ROSES SO PALE?

TRANSLATED FROM THE GERMAN OF HEINE.

Oh! why are the roses so pale,
My love; O! whither has vanished their bloom?
And why, 'mid the grasses that grow in the vale,
Have the violets lost their perfume?

And why have the stars grown so dim,
My love; and the charm of their mystical light
Passed out of the desolate sky, like a dream,
That changes its face in the night?

And why have the music of words,
My love, and the splendors of canvas and pen
Passed away, like the song and flutter of birds,
When the forests have ceased to be green?

Dim to me the sweet light of the skies,
My love, and the glories of nature and art,
When, longing, I see not the light of your eyes,
And feel not the beat of your heart.

Thou whom we cannot see,
Mid all our toil and strife ;
Oh ! Thou who still must be
A presence in our life ;—

Shall we, when near the land
Touched by the mystic river,
Then feel Thy loving hand
To guide and to deliver?

Alas ! we can but guess,
And dimly dream the night
Of death, so dark to us,
May usher in new light,

And yet we fear the night
Too full of clouds may be,
To bring those stars to light,
Which now we cannot see.

Our eyes are filled with tears ;
For they have searched in vain
These many, weary years
Of doubt and toil and pain.

A FRAGMENT.

The frost is on the hills,—and Summer's work is done.
I fain would think that gentle Nature grieves
O'er all the lessening splendors of the setting sun,
The fragile glory of the dropping leaves.

Far over the wide-reaching meadow
  I see the red sun on the bay;
And slowly night's envious shadow
  Will darken the light of the day.

But gladly the sun I surrender,
  For yonder is red-hearted Mars;
And I see that the ravishing splendor
  Was hiding the light of the stars.

A VALENTINE.

The waters kiss the earth so green!
The loving earth and sky embrace,
And yon bright worlds above, I ween,
Keep kissing in the realms of space.

And Night, the goddess eldest born,
The pink of modesty and grace,
Pants for the earliest kiss of morn,
And blushing, hides her starry face.

So now, be thou a gentle giver
Of one sweet gift; for tell me why,
Since all things else are kissing ever,
O, wherefore should not you and I?

TO AN OLD FRIEND.

Seeking labor or pleasure, wherever thou art,
　　Somewhere on the land or the sea :
　　In faith of a promise once made,
Dear friend of my youth and my heart,
　　This greeting I send unto thee.

Away from the shock of alarms,
　　On the edge of the shadowy mere,
　　We have gazed into star-lighted skies,
While the hushed woods lay still in the arms
　　Of the fragrant and motionless air.

Our life is two-fold ; we may tread
　　Its hot sands, while we dream of the green
　　Cool oases now vanished and gone ;
The dead past may uncover its dead—
　　Pale shadows of things that have been.

Ah ! me, must we fail in our quest,
　　Never reach the bright goal that we seek ?

Remorseless the years glide away.
Tired limbs are longing for rest,
  And our voices though tender, are weak.

Sweet rest from the sorrow and pain !
  Sweet rest from the trouble and care !
  But love is unwilling to yield ;
And the spirit hath pinions that fain
  Would beat in a limitless air.

When the day-spring shall pass into night
  And we gaze on the green earth no more,
  May God let me look in thine eyes.
As they smile in the fathomless light,
  That shines on an evergreen shore.

CHRISTMAS DAY, 1870.

Mamma says that the papa must make a few rhymes,
Rhymes, too, that are sensible, pleasant and witty ;
Something to chime with the Christmas chimes,
And carol our love to our dear little Kitty.

And papa has tried and his labor is done.
But he knows, very well, that it is a great pity
These poor little rhymes limp so as they run,
But they 'll carry our love to our dear little Kitty.

The casket is poor, but the jewel is rare.
The casket, you know, is this queer little ditty ;
And the jewel within it is something to wear
Very close to the heart of our dear little Kitty.

The Winter is past. The Summer now comes,
And glad are the faces that smile in our homes.
We wrangle no more over alien rights,
But quaff the bright nectar of friendly delights.

Sharp are the rocks and the brambles we meet;
And lonesome the pathway under our feet.
Brief are the flowers and tender their bloom,
And swift are the storm-winds that steal their
    perfume.

Come out of the shadow and into the light!
Brief is the day and weary the night.
Now touch the sweet lips of child and of wife,
And banish the cares and the sorrows of life.

For each man alike, whether poet or dunce,
The foam on the wine-cup sparkles but once.
Then lift the bright goblet and drink while you
    may—
To-morrow we know not, we live in to-day.

LINES WRITTEN IN A STRANGER'S ALBUM.

I knew a casket rich and rare,
Where Love its sparkling diamonds placed :
And Friendship with a tender care,
Arranged her pearls in faultless taste.

A stranger, *poor in gems,* one day,
Hoping a pleasant smile to win,
Came where the shining casket lay,
And softly dropped a pebble in.

Our faith in things unseen,
So like an unbelief,
Through all our lives has been
Poor solace in our grief.

Oh! we are worn and weary,
Down-trodden in the fight;
Our nights are dark and dreary,
Our days resemble night.

And blindly we must grope
Beneath the barren skies;
We cannot speak of hope,
We will not babble lies.

Thou, whom we cannot find,
Thou, God! concealed from sight,
How shall the weak and blind
E'er stumble into light?

We shall not know Thee here.
We cannot hear Thy voice;
There is no form of prayer
To make our souls rejoice.

Oh! grant that in that hour
When earthly things shall pass,
Behind the clouds that lower,
We may behold Thy face.

LINES TO —— ——

Fair lady, we have met but once—and rapidly
The thoughts and words, that now do crowd
Upon my mind, did fade from out thy memory,
As fades from heaven the passing cloud.

But I could not so soon forget — must ever be
Recalling things too bright to last ;
Must linger over fond remembrances of thee,
Still shining, shining through the past.

O ! would that I could look once more into your
      eyes,
And dream and hope they smiled on me,
Like stars that lovingly look out from Summer
      skies,
To smile upon the trembling sea.

And I would hear once more the music of your
      voice,
That types the music of the heart ;

And feel *my* heart leap up with long-remembered
 joys —
Vague joys that dreams and hopes impart.

But ah ! we ne'er may meet again until the May
Of life shall all have passed and gone ;
Until the blossoms of our youth have passed away,
And wintry age comes stealing on.

But the sweet image of thy face, so briefly known,
And long remembered, still shall dwell
Enshrined within my " heart of hearts " and all
 alone
Be worshipped more than tongue can tell.

How strange is Love ! What golden promises he
 brings,
To thrill us with a wild delight :
And then we only hear the rustling of his wings,
As he unfurls them for his flight.

And now, farewell!   I know these feeble lines are
    naught
To thee.   But still it must belong
To Love, " thus silvered over with the cast of
    thought,"
To breathe its passion forth in song.

GROWING OLD.

From success in its pride and defeat in its shame,
From the later repose, and the earlier strife,
The half that we learn is but knowledge in name,
And dark is the myst'ry that broods over life.

I smile at the hopes and the dreams of my youth —
Brief splendors of morning with clouds overcast!
Yet something of worth, which I cling to, in sooth,
Have I wrung from the vanishing years as they
    passed.

I have painfully tested the Old and the New,
Learned what to distrust and what to believe;
Gained a knowledge of things that are steadfast
    and true,
And a knowledge of things that will cheat and
    deceive;

Of the uncertain fame of the pen and the sword;

Of the pride that arises from ill-gotten gain :
Of the glory of labor that seeks no reward,
But silently carries its burden of pain ;

Of the courage that faces and tramples on death ;
Of the garrulous grief, which time will assuage ;
Of the bubbles that sparkle and break with a breath ;
Of the love that grows warmer and sweeter with
    age ;

Of the valor that turns from a glittering cause,
In the day and the hour of its noisy success,
To worship the strength and the stillness of laws,
That endure through the ages and æons that pass.

But alas ! for the knowledge that comes with the
    flight
Of the hours ; for a sorrowful thing 'tis to know
Of the increasing shadow and lessening light,
As the days and the months and the years come
    and go.

The friends of my boyhood and youth, one by one,
And the friends that my manhood held dear, like
    the gleams
Of a warm, sweet summer remembered, have gone
Quite out of my life, and into my dreams.

And the glow, and the wealth of the morning have
    passed,
And the fullness of noon grown empty and cold;
And I feel all the sadness that must come at last,
Of thoughts that are barren, and limbs that are old.

Yet I welcome the sadness, and weakness of limb,
For I know that the lights from the City of Rest,
Shine clearer to him whose eyes have grown dim
In watching the shadows that grow in the West.

POEM.

READ BEFORE THE GRAFTON AND COOS COUNTIES BAR ASSOCIATION AT LANCASTER, 1884.

Before reading my exercise, I am inclined to make a few preliminary remarks. I have nothing to say about the quality of the composition which I hold in my hand, at least in prose. I have said what I wished to say on that subject in rhyme. I am perfectly willing that anybody should regard my effort as a great and original poem. I shall make no quarrel with the generous critic upon that point; but I desire to apologize for the brevity of the article. It is a novel theme for apology, certainly, but I think a good one. I met Brother Batchellor at the late term of court in Concord, and he informed me that I had been appointed Bard of the Association. I was somewhat frightened. In the first place, I hadn't any very distinct idea what a Bard was; and then I couldn't understand what the Association wanted of a Bard. But I found excuses were not in order. Brother Batchellor told me that nobody was permitted to decline an honor thrust upon him by the Association. And so I agreed to try. I have done what I could; but I have been cramped for time, and I have had on my hands other duties, which could not be put aside. Moreover, my Pegasus is getting old, and his wind is short, and he never was much of a traveller. He is accustomed to make short journeys at long intervals. Indeed he reminds me very much of a certain horse my father used to own. The horse was named Sullen, and he was a very peculiar animal. He would travel when he chose to travel, and no amount of persuasion, however violent, could induce him to travel when he did not chose. When the humor struck him, he would stop in the middle of a wide, smooth, level, unobstructed road, and you might whip him, kick him, knock him down or build a fire under him, without any perceptible effect upon his locomotion. My father always used to provide himself with a book or newspaper whenever he went out to drive the creature, and when the horse stopped, the driver would begin to read, and would continue to read, sometimes for hours, until at last the idea would get into the head of the horse, that possibly, all things considered, some moderate degree of progress might be preferable to the monotony of a long-continued state of rest.

To-day, they tell me, I must speak in rhyme,

And, hoping for the coming of the time,

When rhymed conduct, deeds in harmony

With generous impulse, in nobility

Of thought conceived, beyond our present reach,

May take the place of music in our speech,

I yield to other's wishes, and rehearse

A mass of barren platitudes in verse.

Therefore, my lyre, thy mute and tuneless strings

Must tremble at the touch of one who sings,

When he should only talk, and strives to bring

Back to dead leaves the greenness of the spring.

Like the huge bird that shakes its useless wings,
Then runs, and backward worthless rubbish flings,
My thoughts prosaic, poor and common things,
I scatter, strung upon poetic strings.

But let me speak a word of honest praise,
Regardless of the mocking, bitter lays
Of many a rhymster in the by-gone days.
For we who know our noble calling best,
Can well afford to let the vulgar jest
Pass pointless by us, like the idle wind,
Since they who shut their eyes must needs be
blind.
But who, I ask, are those, who never pause
In faithful service, ne'er betray a cause,
Whose plighted word, with great affairs at stake,
No cautious lawyer e'er declined to take,
But looks upon a verbal promise given,
As something sacred as his hope of heaven?
Who do no falsehood, nor consent that lies
Be hidden from the calm and patient eyes

Of Justice, never wittingly promote,
Or sue, or help, a false, unlawful suit.
Nor e'er, by hint, or look, or deed, or word,
Consent that any such false cause be heard?
For lucre or for malice will delay
No man, but justly give to each his day
In Court, with due fidelity to all,
The slaves of Justice, though the heavens should
    fall?

My brothers, ye, who seek the holy grail
By swearing this, in words that must not fail.
Behold the shining goal at which we aim;
And if, o'er th' rough uneven soil with lame
And halting steps, we stumble now and then,
We lose not hope, but stumble like brave men,
Who struggle o'er an upward sloping land,
And falling, take another firmer stand.
And nobly strive their former place to gain,
Or e'en an out-look from a loftier plane,
Nor shed unmanly tears o'er hopeless pain.

The time is brief, but " hear me for my cause."
I speak in reverence of the holy laws,
Not always easy to be seen and read,
But stern in their demands to be obeyed,
Not always to be found in printed books,
(Sermons in stones, and in the running brooks,)
Transcribed upon the tablets of the heart,
And legible to those who have the art
Of spelling out their rich, mysterious lore.
My brothers! Ye whose aims may sink or soar,
Who cannot pass your lives in dreamful ease,
Whose paths can never be the paths of peace,
Who fight for all the prizes that ye win ;
Above the rushing tumult and the din
Of battle, hear the poet of our time,
Singing low, " we can make our lives sublime."

I turn from this exalted theme,
Strong in the hope that it may never seem
To us or others but a dazzling dream,
To glance a moment at the present good,

Of binding fast the bonds of 'brotherhood,
Helping each other in and out of Court,
In all things comely and of good report.
Beyond this public pledge we must not go:
Our rightful homage first is due unto
The cause we serve,—he who commands our aid,
Must keep the narrow road we hope to tread.
I pass not by the good of goodly cheer;
For we are those, who have no lurking fear,
That all the flowery paths of life must tend
Sheer downward to a melancholy end,
And land the luckless traveller where
His soul must be beyond the reach of prayer.
Who walk in duty's path, what'er betides,
May pluck the flowers that blossom on its sides.

We justly boast that our fraternity
Is true and genuine democracy,
And so we stand upon the level earth,
And judge men by their measured worth,
And all the glory and the pride of birth,

The insolence of office, show of wealth,
Are naught to us compared with rugged health
Of body and of soul ; we look the race
Of men and women squarely in the face ;
We never scorn a man of low estate,
Nor bow the knee in worship of the great.
We reach the hand of fellowship to all,
Whose hearts are sound, whose heads are not too
    small.
For us, ascetic virtues have no charm,
Our vision is too dull to see the harm
That lurks in harmless things, and being free,
We grant and take a generous liberty.
I sing, if not the over-flowing bowl,
The feast of reason and the flow of soul,
The quips and quirks, and genial repartees,
Bubbles that float upon a mind at ease,
And wit, that comes unbidden and unsought,
And shimmers o'er a grave and noble thought,
Like the green sward upon a rocky lea,
Or sunlight on the bosom of the sea.

And sometimes in the smooth and burnished gold
Of bright and funny narratives well told,
Which like good wine improve by growing old,
We'll see our own queer faces when we're sold.
And thus we'll while away an hour at ease,
Forgetting all the wretched similes,
About the ants and little busy bees,
Forgetting all our weary toil and strife,
With open hands to grasp the sweets of life,
With open hearts to take in all the good
There is in frank and honest brotherhood,
And grateful hearts to that mysterious power,
That lives in Nature now and evermore,
Must meet us when our little lives shall cease,
And where " beyond these voices there is peace."

SELECTIONS.

SELECTIONS.

DETACHED THOUGHTS.

Can any man tell me, why we should suppress a hearty laugh in this world, because we are blessed with a hope that in some better world we may possibly find some better employment?

There are two classes of believers in this world;—and I acknowledge a kindly feeling towards both of them. Those who open their eyes and look for themselves into the mysterious workings of the Higher Law, into what has been called the "open secret," and see or think that they see,—and those who do not themselves see, but believe in those who say that *they* can see.

I submit to you that there is a show of reason in what a man says, when he says this : "It all looks dark to me, but how is it that Shakespeare, and Goethe, and Dante, and Milton, and Swedenborg were believers? Did not their deeper vision detect a harmony, where there is discord to me?"

I quarrel with no man's creed. Demanding considerable freedom myself in order to be made comfortable, I am disposed to be tolerant to others. The more a man believes, the better, perhaps, if his belief will only help him in his desperate and sometimes disastrous conflict with the Powers of Evil. Still I think it is better to believe a little intensely than a great deal doubtfully.

Permit me to say one word in favor of a large-minded, liberal tolerance of opinion—a tolerance, worthy not only of a conscientious, but an enlightened community. Trust me. one man has just as good a right as another, to hold on to an innocent belief, moral, religious, political or scientific, provided he behaves himself.

We never need be alarmed at the perilous situation of truth. Of all the things in this world, that is the one thing which is best capable of taking care of itself.

It is indeed true that our religion has, *to a certain extent*, ceased to be a " worship of the Beautiful, practice of the Good, pursuit of the True," and become *to a certain other extent*, a cunningly devised piece of machinery, by means of which, without the harsh necessity of a well spent life, we may shun the horrors of one place, and embrace the delights of another.

And then our charity which is the best part of our religion, and which ought to be as unrestricted as the sunlight, how it withdraws the light of its countenance, even from them, who, with different badges, bow at the same shrine, commit the same sins, and plead for the same redemption.

———— —— ——

It has always appeared to me that Nature, although patient and long-suffering enough, is in the end, extremely sure-footed in the administration of her penalties. She never scatters them with a careless hand. They never come, unless in the wake of a violated law.

————————

The poetical element in human life is something like that strange plant that flowers of its own accord, once in a hundred years. It has been well said, that your poet must be a man of richer, purer, nobler nature than other men. Providence sees fit, at rare intervals, to send such a man among us, and when sent, *he* makes poetry, even as the sun shines, or the trees grow, or the birds sing, or the buds blossom—just because it is his nature to do it. Poesy has ever sung and will ever sing its own wild, sweet song. its own wild way, and in its own good time ; and you cannot place fetters upon it, or force it into an unnatural activity by any mechanical process known to the money changers or the committee men.

In the name of all that is the most precious in life, in the name of all that deserves to be immortal, let us try to render sacred by concealment the little good we do. The benefits that flow from our little lives are hardly worth talking about, and if remembered at all, are better preserved in the memory of others than of ourselves.

Possibly it is not altogether a figure of speech to represent music as an angel—a messenger, sent to us from some other world, and bringing with her something of the glory of her real home. And I, for one, will welcome her all the more warmly, that she comes to us, not as the representative of a partial creed, but rather as the representative of an universal belief—that she speaks to us not in the dialect of a sect, but in the language of our common humanity. Coming from afar, she stoops to play with us, to smile with us, to laugh with us, to weep with us, and yet her main office is to speak with us in her sweet, mystic language of the mysteries that lie beyond us.

Liberty is always the child of discipline. They alone are free who are most hopelessly bound, but whose chains and fetters do not chafe them. Freedom from salutary and necessary restraint — the privilege of shaking off solemn obligations which have been voluntarily assumed — the right to walk in any other than the narrow path of duty,—can these constitute Liberty ?

The world has progressed somewhat. The nightmare of superstition has been shaken off, and heresy is no longer a crime. By a long course of bloody instructions, we have been slowly taught that we cannot impair a man's faith or convince his reason by torturing his body,—that even a pestilential heresy will be nourished by the blood of its martyrs.

I know of nothing that interferes with the growth of a healthy morality so much as a long list of artificial sins.

In the hurry and rush and tumult of business, we sometimes lose sight of those eternal laws which underlie all private and public well-being. In the broad glare of day, you know, the stars *seem* to go out ; but they are there in the heavens all the same, and it is no evidence that they are extinguished, that the light of a nearer sun floods our dull eyes, so that we cannot see those far-off, still-shining stars.

In that dark hour, which follows us all with a stealthy and ever-increasing pace ; in that dark hour,

when the shadows of some other world will come
falling thick around us, all our loud and empty protes-
tations of superior virtue, all the miserable quackery
of our whole lives, will be forgotten, or painfully
remembered; and our simple deeds of kindness, our
unseen acts of charity will come forth from the twi-
light of memory, radient even as the stars come forth,
when day is passing into the solemn night.

www.ingramcontent.com/pod-product-compliance
Lightning Source LLC
Chambersburg PA
CBHW031752090426
42739CB00008B/989